WIND OVER STONES

ALSO BY ADELE KENNY

Poetry
- *Not Asking What If*
- *A Lightness, A Thirst, or Nothing at All*
- *What Matters*
- *The Kite & Other Poems from Childhood*
- *Chosen Ghosts*
- *Illegal Entries*
- *An Archaeology of Ruins*
- *At the Edge of the Woods*
- *Starship Earth*
- *Castles and Dragons*
- *Questi Momenti*
- *Migrating Geese*
- *Between Hail Marys*
- *The Roses Open*
- *Notes from the Nursing Home*

Nonfiction
- *Chapbooks: A Historical Perspective*
- *Staffordshire Figures: History in Earthenware 1740–1900*
- *Photographic Cases: Victorian Design Sources 1840–1870*
- *Staffordshire Animals: A Collector's Guide*
- *Staffordshire Spaniels: A Collector's Guide*
- *We Become By Being*
- *The Silence and the Flame: Clare and Francis of Assisi*
- *Counseling Gifted, Creative, and Talented Youth Through the Arts*
- *A Creative Writing Companion*

WIND OVER STONES

EKPHRASTIC PROSE POEMS

Adele Kenny

Welcome Rain Publishers
NEW YORK

Copyright © 2019 by Adele Kenny

All rights reserved. Except for brief passages quoted in reviews, no part of this book may be reproduced in any form or by any means for any purpose without permission in writing from the author.

Welcome Rain Publishers, LLC
217 Thompson Street, #473
New York, New York 10012

www.welcomerain.com

ISBN-13: 978-1-56649-405-2
ISBN-10: 1-56649-405-2

Library of Congress Cataloging Data is available.

Cover Art: *The Rocks* by Vincent van Gogh
Book design by Smythtype Design

In Memory of
Linda Radice & Gail Gerwin

*There are special people in our lives who never leave us—
even after they are gone.*

—D. Morgan

Painting is silent poetry,
and poetry is painting that speaks.

—SIMONIDES

CONTENTS

I

Evening as Footnote   2
    After *Evening Wind* by Edward Hopper

How Things Were   3
    After *Children's Games* by Pieter Brueghel the Elder

What You See   4
    After *The Somnambulist* by Sir John Everett Millais

Even When She Isn't Sure, She Is   5
    After *Winter Landscape* by Eugène Henri Paul Gauguin

Of What Is   6
    After *Woman before the Setting Sun* by Caspar David Friedrich

On Dit   7
    After *Cats* by Natalia Goncharova

She Kept the Theory Going…   8
    After *Femme aux Phlox* by Albert Gleizes

This Almost Night   9
    After *Man and Woman Contemplating the Moon* by Caspar David Friedrich

Old Wine or Misfortune   10
    After *The Green Mirror* by Guy Rose

Whatever Title We Gave It   11
    After *Enchantment (Cinderella)* by Maxfield Parrish

It Doesn't Take Much   12
    After *Lesbia and Her Sparrow* by Sir Edward John Poynter

As If That Place   13
    After *Landscape: Garden Path* by Marie Bracquemond

II

For a Moment, Like Stones After *The Wave* by Pierre-August Renoir	16
Seeing and Seeing After *The False Mirror* by René Magritte	17
If I'm Searching Again After *Beech Grove* by Gustav Klimt	18
In Memory Of After *Beata Beatrix* by Dante Gabriel Rossetti	19
Because This Name Will Stop with Me… After *A Family* by Louis le Brocquy	20

Once, Late in the Day
    After *Mountain Landscape with Bridge*
    by Thomas Gainsborough
	21

Just Perhaps After *Ophelia* by John Everett Millais	22
The Part After *The Weeping Woman* by Pablo Picasso	23
Pieces After *Forget Me Not* by Arthur Hughes	24
What She's Always Known After *Flaming June* by Sir Frederic Leighton	25
Poem about Angels that Begins with a Sump Pump After *Head of an Angel* by Vincent van Gogh	26
Moment and Memory After *Starry Night* by Jean-François Millet	27

III

Simply Here   30
    After *Epiphany* by Max Ernst

Where the Dead Are Strangers   31
    After *All Souls' Day* by Jakub Schikaneder

Past the Waterline   32
    After *Lake with Dead Trees* by Thomas Cole

For a Long Time   33
    After *Pilgrim at the Gate of Idleness* by Edward Burne-Jones

Shooting Stars   34
    After *Tintagel on the Cornish Coast* by W. T. Richards

A Man at the Desk   35
    After *Still Life with an Open Book and Spectacles* by William T. Howell Allchin

What Becomes   36
    After *Montagne Sainte-Victoire* by Paul Cézanne

This Particular Light   37
    After *The Sun* by Edvard Munch

So Here You Are   38
    After *Spring* by Georgia O'Keeffe

If There Is Such a Thing   39
    After *Woman by a Window Feeding Her Dog* by Mary Cassatt

The Way   40
    After *Night Scene* by Peter Paul Rubens

Just Enough Spectacle   41
    After *Snow Scene at Argenteuil* by Claude Monet

Good Enough   42
    After *The Great Pine* by Paul Cézanne

As Far as Here Goes	43
After *Soul of the Rose* by John William Waterhouse	
We Can Only Ask	44
After *Our Lady of Peace* by Evelyn de Morgan	
Like Wind Over Stones	45
After *The Rocks* by Vincent van Gogh	
The Paintings	47
Notes	69
Acknowledgments	71
About the Author	73

> QR codes are included in this book so that readers can access the paintings that inspired the poems while they are reading. This interactive element enables readers to enjoy a multi-dimensional experience through their smart phones with cameras or free QR code scanning applications on their mobile devices.

WIND
OVER
STONES

I

*We must let go of the life we planned,
so as to accept the one that is waiting for us.*

—JOSEPH CAMPBELL

Evening as Footnote
>(After *Evening Wind* by Edward Hopper)

Evening as footnote after the long day's rain: unfolded curtains move in and out of the window—second wing of the same dream—one bird, the sky otherwise empty.

My friend Joe writes, *A little drooping death never hurt a poor boy.* Joe grew up poor. We both did—you get used to things that equal loss.

When you stand and look up, the night sky fills with memories of stars no longer there, and a voice (just over your shoulder) asks, *Where are you?*

How Things Were
    (After Pieter Brueghel the Elder's *Children's Games*)

It's about the wonder of what we thought, and something about not paying attention because we didn't have to—it's about how things changed. After we ducked and took cover in hallways (just as the film taught us), we faced the wall and stood in tight lines—away from the windows—left arms raised and folded in front of our foreheads, right hands at the back of our necks. These were the school air raid drills and we (50s kids) had no idea what bombs were or why we did this.

Post-war children, the only soldiers we understood were green plastic, my cousin Eddie's army, half of which we tossed into the storm sewer (and then our comic books so they'd have something to read). We didn't know about our fathers' war, never feared a sky darkened by enemy planes, and had no idea what "nuclear" would come to mean. The drills were something we did as much by rote as arithmetic and spelling. By second or third grade, they stopped. As far as we knew, there *was* no end of the world, no end of anything—life was nothing more than how things were—our innocence an amulet, a green plastic soldier, that kept us safe.

What You See
> (After *The Somnambulist* by Sir John Everett Millais)

But always the time other than now—deep into being and not (a kind of detached waiting). Balanced on a ledge of memory's spectrum, she knows more than she needed to know—the loss after each loss that doesn't go away. It's come to this: everything measured—before, after—the way life never goes back to life as it used to be—and how much dark we need to see the stars.

In twilight's ribbed light, the distance is twilled with gray, the sky reordered. A ghost-bird calls over the cliffs. Its voice falls into the sea like a soul's final word as it leaves the body. Her candle sputters in its last bit of tallow. No moon. No stars. She walks slowly into what may or may not be a dream—a deeper mirror, herself inside it.

Even When She Isn't Sure, She Is
    (After *Winter Landscape* by Eugène Henri Paul Gauguin)

Not the sky flashed out in stars, or night's snapped sheet—not what's frozen or how deep this winter is. A woodpecker taps into its own sound, everything else unspoken. She knows how dark gone is, and fear (always there) just under the surface.

Like other abstractions—wherever we go, what's left and what's not—a stretched shadow, the snow's reckoning—things never as much or as little as we think.

She says she is sure and surely not, says she is this: the sharp edge of a laugh, whatever the cold brings in.

Of What Is

(After *Woman before the Setting Sun*
by Caspar David Friedrich)

She tells herself she's not much changed—only the details and what she knows but, of course, she knows better.

What passes here will pass as surely as the old dog's bones beneath her garden stone—anything left is holy: the way light falls in empty rooms, how even sunlight rustles in fall. It's the way she stays the same as she was and different—a thin line where the river used to be.

It's how she treasures the never-used (a silver tea set, a painted plate), the voice she almost remembers and how it connects waking to sleep—her own small echo that goes unheard.

On Dit

(After Cats *by Natalia Goncharova)*

It's said that she's crazy, that she rarely leaves her house but moves curtains to let the sun in and raises windows when the moon trails light. Sometimes, the dog she named for a poet barks inside (if you listen, you'll hear him).

She has no faith in memory (what she doesn't know, she can't forget). There's enough in what is. She understands the hard line of broken things—the ones with names and not (feeling and fringe), how certainty and uncertainty equal the same damned thing—what adds up, what doesn't (the heart's weight, what's left in the flesh).

She says, *Let the bird's black wing stay in the black sky (just as it is)—a cat in disguise (its claws out)—that bird, that sky (the moon strung in its cycle of tides—poor moon, poor sky). No other sightings—it's what happens when grief becomes the way we love.*

She Kept the Theory Going…
                (After *Femme aux Phlox* by Albert Gleizes)

through all of it—things that lasted, things that didn't—the long, slow now of whatever was, whatever happened. So much history.

Chipmunks and squirrels come to the deck for peanuts and bread…cardinals, jays…among them, how perfectly plain the plain brown sparrows. She picks the last blue phlox from the garden. The gazebo is quiet. Such peace as there is.

Twilight falls in shaded planes. Cicada shells crumble in the ivy. She's willing to be wrong. Willing to suspend belief and disbelief, even the in-built practice of doubt. From every angle, the moon is unbeamed. Higher up, the archer nocks an arrow onto his bow—galaxies burn around him.

This Almost Night
                (After *Man and Woman Contemplating the Moon*
                                     by Caspar David Friedrich)

It's the way trees darken before the sky…this almost night…another side of time and new. We think in pauses and, in those pauses, everything (it seems) stands still.

The moon, rising, reorders the sky, drifts and slips through clouds—sliver of moon, its nimbus pale, like a word almost spoken.

A night bird lifts its shadow away from the world, a world flown white with the ghosts of our passing (thoughts vaguely remembered)—the sky dimmed to November gray, and us moonstruck—what we thought we knew, fistfuls of winter we didn't see coming, this sack of rocks slung over memory's shoulder.

Old Wine or Misfortune
>(After *The Green Mirror* by Guy Rose)

November smudged underfoot, but all those stars: everything else impossible or gone—the way we passed through each other—light through water. You would call it old wine or misfortune—so long ago, I can't remember what the promise looked like—as if it never happened. And there's nothing left in that last moment of memory—a star committed to its own vanishing, already burned out, as if I imagined it. One of us looked up, one of us looked away.

Whatever Title We Gave It
    (After *Enchantment, aka Cinderella* by Maxfield Parrish)

A beak in the throat or stones in a metal pail—the song doesn't matter (whatever title we gave it, however we thought we would sing it—the way we learned to circle illusions). What should have been star-strung mythologized into something that never was, an occluded fairy tale (the fabricated kind intended to deceive): the glass shoe in a thousand pieces—words left out—that kind of ending.

It Doesn't Take Much
    (After *Lesbia and Her Sparrow* by Sir Edward John Poynter)

Mid-February—sparrows huddle on the window ledge, and not even they know which will make it to spring. It works like that—where weathers and decisions take us—one afternoon on the steps of the Lido Diner and you there (reading your *Soldier of Fortune* magazine). It must have been late July or August, heat deep in the leaves (the sun that hot), everything more than I could imagine.

I was never quite sure who you were, how much was plotted or chance (and all the impossible identities we assumed). You said you knew I'd be the one to turn away. I didn't believe you; I didn't believe *them* when they told me you were dead. Sometimes, when I close my eyes deeply, I remember how I felt.

It doesn't take much: the *was* in *what is*—the way behind unchanged—how a forest grew up out of your grave, the sparrow I wear on my wrist as if it had all been real.

As If That Place
    (After *Landscape: Garden Path* by Marie Bracquemond)

As if that place were a language no longer spoken, details remembered like glyphs on a limestone wall—a long indelible then. And one season (between spring and summer), written in the half-time of who we were—before the burden of seeing changed us. Mistakable us—no thought to the hands our fingers made or who we would become—what we lacked in our lives, we lacked in ourselves. But here, from this vantage ("then" too far away to be redeemed), there is still the brightness (and order) that memory claims—lanes of bloodroot and blue star, the sun's deep light scratched into stones.

II

*Between our life and death we may touch understanding,
As a moth brushes a window with its wing.*

—CHRISTOPHER FRY

For a Moment, Like Stones
   (After *The Wave* by Pierre-August Renoir)

Terrified or indifferent, having taken enough chances—all things at once (and then, regret)—it's easy to forget what we're here for (easy to become like every unreadable thing and the moon that has no light of its own). There are no equivalents, only what falls by accident or master plan.

Like everything brief, anything provisional, we stand on afterthought—the balance point of when—a place of half spaces and scattered distractions. Awakened from dreams that don't make sense, we measure time in immediate history (what belongs to us, what's not returned).

Transients here, awkward and sad, we trust in mysteries and barely know ourselves. Like Icarus, we create whatever flight we can, glimpse our shadows on the wave below and float… for a moment, like stones.

Seeing and Seeing
                    (After *The False Mirror* by René Magritte)

It's any thought where the mind is—welter and well—light trailed through flat black. In this dream, she combs the wind with her hands, an eye on the tip of each finger, evidence of you are—seeing and seeing—formed in a frame of blue sky (blue as the blue sky is). She remembers this sidewalk (so many cracks), and the thud of sun on stone. It's summer and hot. She's four, maybe five, not asking what if or what anything. She doesn't know those words, no one has told her (and if there's a lesson in that, she learned it well). She thinks of Peter Pan, of flying; and, then, the awful ticking—the swallowed clock. She wakes just as the dream becomes literal—what isn't, what is.

If I'm Searching Again
(After *Beech Grove* by Gustav Klimt)

It was only then that I came close: not in the dreams themselves, or even in what they meant—a thousand knives deep and so many sleepless nights. I should have known. It's the way wind pulls leaves and they fall, how we tire and fail (we *all* fail)—and, always, this fear of anything unpredictable, the randomness in loss—one after another (even the voluntary dead—their refusal to stay alive).

Tonight, the street narrows. I'm running. I don't know why I dream this or what I run from (if not my own lineage, if not the pale girl on the iceberg). Out of nowhere, trees snap from their roots. I'm alone inside a dark arcade; damp air shawls across my back. On the street outside, my father's Harley spins out, and he's underneath (the .44 mag in one hand, his badge in the other). Boots scrape on the pavement—sparks shoot up from under their heels, sulphur and soot in the air. The sky blank and black. I think of Pompeii—how it was for them—the old gods' wrath, or no gods left—a place of ghosts just watching the clock, just watching.

If I'm searching again (and I must be), I know you're there (somewhere beyond the disfigured trees, their soft wood in your arms). I reach for pieces, as close to breath as I can get—as close to a dream that hope still clings to, even if only by rote, by nothing more than what it remembers.

In Memory Of
               (After *Beata Beatrix* by Dante Gabriel Rossetti)

No movement but this: subdued luminosity, sunlight from the distant city. River. Bridge. There is always a background (that far, this close), and what memory does—like the dusky lines of a double shadow, it multiplies loss.

In Rossetti's *Beata*, a sundial casts its metal wing on the thin, blown hour when leaving begins. Red dove, white poppy: the woman, transfixed, slips—diffused like light through darkened glass—her hands open and soft.

I am here and you aren't. It is summer—the sky is clapper and bell, the lemonade sweet. I can almost hear you singing.

Because This Name Will Stop with Me...
                       (After *A Family* by Louis le Brocquy)

the poem stops here and holds its breath. Family names (bone and blood-line) told in brogue float like ghosts around me—portable fates that speak of Aengus and Oisín. Somewhere, far from here, the lucky and unloved lie side-by-side—what still exists, what story is (spring and evening as they used to be). Distant, in another room, a clock (already handed down four times) still ticks and chimes a half-turn past the moon, inside the crickets' hack and saw—a sound that is voice (that is time), like glass inside a bell that rings as if through rain.

Once, Late in the Day:
East Canada Creek, Stratford, NY
(After *Mountain Landscape with Bridge*
by Thomas Gainsborough)

I've come to see the sun flick over stones in moments of gentle flashing, to think how fast a memory becomes its own illusion. I'm here because what we call the soul—that almost visual echo—is always close to holiness.

A birch on the shoreline shapes itself to the breeze; aspens tremble as if this moment were all there is between one beauty and another, between mystery and revelation. Here, there is no revision, no opposite for recollection.

Once, late in the day, my father and I fished beneath this bridge. I was seven or eight, and small trout shone underwater, quietly golden. On the only road home, we were part of the shadows' perfection (trees and what was left of the sky). As we walked between hills (close in the last light), my pail of water filled with stars, and the sun came down, fallen from a larger light that, far too soon, my father walked into and was gone.

Just Perhaps

(After *Ophelia* by John Everett Millais)

Buoyed by her dress, she barely breaks the water's surface—arms outstretched, palms upturned. Pansies float above her skirt. There are daisies on the glassy stream, and, there (to the left, above her head), a bird on the pollard from which she jumped or fell. Broken willow, broken bough.

And just perhaps, as Hamlet's mother said, she's still alive and singing—see, her mouth is open, and her eyes; and just perhaps, she doesn't know how close to death she is—or why this painting makes me think of you. *Your* death was not offstage the way Ophelia's was (the ladder placed, the rope around your neck); nor was the way you parted from yourself, the silent swinging—only air beneath your feet.

The Part
                  (After *The Weeping Woman* by Pablo Picasso)

The little girl knew an evil man who touched her, terrified her; and she didn't tell anyone, not even her mother—no one, until the week before she died when she told her daughter. She said the memory was vague, but always there—like a brief, back-cover description of someone else's book.

She wasn't sure who the man was (uncle or family friend). She couldn't remember how many times or exactly where, just an almost-suppressed memory of his face, his voice: *Don't tell anyone, your parents won't love you if you tell.* She said his breath smelled like spoiled milk.

Into the valley of wicked men—she was four, maybe five, and grew up thinking she was ugly. My mother—always beautiful to me—who learned how to cry silently (no prayer to revision or apology), tears sewn into her eyes for the rest of her life. And me, these long years later, still guilty for what I might have said but didn't, for not knowing how to reach the part of her that stayed broken, the part that didn't tell.

Pieces

(After *Forget Me Not* by Arthur Hughes)

I set aside pieces of furniture, clothing, more books than my own shelves can hold—the ones she loved most and titled spines I remember from childhood, can see even now with my eyes closed. I place DuMaurier's *Frenchman's Creek* into a carton marked "keep" and wrap her jewelry box to take with me (as if any one of those small, bright rings on my own finger might bring her hands back into being).

The sky goes dark, loosely draped with white night-clouds. Stars gather in windows scored with memories of light that burned out long before any of us was here. Shadows pass through the edge of sight—a sigh, a laugh hauntingly far away. I pack dresses and shoes, take down the last of the hangars and close the door to her bedroom. There's no way back to what was, only these rooms filled with new silence, a house to be emptied and sold.

It's true that we lose their voices first (inflection, tone), and I haven't learned how to reconcile this listening with the voice I can no longer hear. There's no formula for letting go of the old, gone world or this house where every ordinary thing has become more than it is.

What She's Always Known
                (After *Flaming June* by Sir Frederic Leighton)

Having lived through it twice herself, having lost her mother to it, she says her friend's diagnosis is a sledgehammer (one of those appropriate clichés that, even so, still fails). So many fractions, so many sorrows. This friend…this autumn…

She dreams the old, recurrent dream—a boardwalk parallel to the sea, the sea slurred. A piece of rosewood reaches between waves like a polished arm. The lighthouse is down, the sky fire and salt. Sound ricochets from the shooting gallery; a carousel races, music stretched to a tinny wail, and then (always unexpected, at first peripheral) something dark and fast—a sudden claw on the last brass ring—what life has taken was never hers to give.

Poem about Angels That Begins with a Sump Pump
(After *Head of an Angel* by Vincent van Gogh)

Whenever it rains hard, I remember a torrential day when it seemed the downpour would never stop. How I worried about the sump pump—if it worked properly or worked at all. Late that day, I raced home to a flooded cellar. The pump wheezed and buzzed under inches of water that covered the floor. I was standing in it when the sparks started. Afraid to pull the plug, knowing what might happen, I did it anyway—my breath held against one, last electrical surge that might have killed me. I spent that night bailing and mopping, sweeping water into the French drain (also known as *a weeping drain*).

Of course, worse things have happened, much worse. I didn't think of angels then: guardian angels, angels of lost causes, angels of what I meant to say and never did—not even my own angel (I've written about him before), the old one who wheezes in with a sound like the sump pump. A marble angel who crawls out of stone in heavy benediction. Never quite luminous, his wings creak and beat at oblique angles—all that flapping between his invisible world and mine—he's hardly celestial. Angel with a body, body of an angel. Tracked through sky and sky (when his own weight escapes him), he's musty, ephemeral, but he loves me the way people need to be loved—without pretense, without lies—and he flies toward me (always at the last minute), wrists like bells ringing, a miracle in each fist. This is the angel of all my worst uncertainties, the angel who never speaks but stands behind me, the one with his hand on my shoulder when I say, *I'm not sure*—his hand on my shoulder when I say *I believe.*

Moment and Memory
                    (After *Starry Night* by Jean-François Millet)

Moment and memory, accidental dreams…and right now, hummingbirds, bee balm; a blue hydrangea against the fence (the easiness of it—complete simplicity). Outside, dusk settles. My dog sleeps on his pillow beside me. In the yard next door, a neighbor child sings, her nursery rhyme high and sweet through my half-closed window, carried in on the same breeze that moves between my hands.

Night falls and fills with katydids. Shooting stars, (momentary) like the last sparrows and finches, are a mismatched flock that moves the sky. Limitless world. We learn the space between endings and beginnings (so much to number and know)—the continuum always unfinished.

III

Your life is shaped by the end you live for.

—THOMAS MERTON

Simply Here

                        (After *Epiphany* by Max Ernst)

No one told us the shepherds' names (the dishonored, the thieves). And no one knows what star the Magi followed (which king brought Frankincense, which brought myrrh—how much holy gold). Who knows what they thought of the cobbled sky or, if (after finally seeing), their bodies went into the distance without them—sheep like clouds on far-off fields.

Deep inside the wind's white dream, a river stills. There's more snow pending…that coming and coming again…What is here is simply here, where we are—where we've been headed all along—and light everywhere.

Where the Dead Are Strangers
>(After *All Souls' Day* by Jakub Schikaneder)

Past what we see, a river glistens with wind and sun. A bird rises above its wings and recedes into sky. Deer graze between stones where the forest is close, a tangle of underbrush and leaves. One tomb's shadow reaches into another's.

Eyes filled with burdens (so much to do), we come to this place where the dead are strangers—where there is no ache of ghosts—the wages of grief only scrub grass and weeds that call us to something beyond ourselves, something exact and perfect, more absolute than the earth.

Past the Waterline
     (After *Lake with Dead Trees* by Thomas Cole)

This could be any day, anywhere—either one of us could be the other, momentary deer where the water ends and the forest begins. Whatever hard things we've seen—what we've fallen under—remind us of the way wind strips the pines, how dark gathers and thins the light. Dead limbs rest on stretched water, above and within their own reflections. Memory re-collects itself beyond the surface. We listen and, listening, hear the voice inside that becomes its own spirit. Past the waterline and the tree line, we move between *all* lines to a pause that is neither time nor now—the purest *here* as our minds pass through it.

For a Long Time
(After *Pilgrim at the Gate of Idleness* by Edward Burne-Jones)

She's thought about this for a long time, drew the lines (backward, forward) and crossed them. It was always about getting things right, and not—a wanting to be—never quite what she intended.

She lived for years with all the missing things—with every green ghost that spoke of was, and she held the dead close to keep them from slipping away completely. *Now, she says, something more than the visible world.*

The last hope is the best hope. On her windowsill, violet sprigs stand in a glass of water, their new roots almost transparent.

Shooting Stars
    (After *Tintagel on the Cornish Coast* by W. T. Richards)

High on the headland, castle ruins sink into shadow. Some say Arthur was born here—mystery and myth—a romantic notion that may or may not be real. At low tide, Merlin's Cave opens below. Far above, a kestrel rests on an updraft then lowers itself in stages; the horizon loses shape. It is August and night—darkness shot through with unfastened light. The wind picks up and becomes weightless—even these stones are made of air.

As it was in the beginning, is now and ever shall be—more than moment, more than idea. (A cobweb brushes against my cheek.) How little we know of our own smallness—of rock and dust—how little we know of ghosts, of stars.

A Man at the Desk
>(After *Still Life with an Open Book and Spectacles*
>by William T. Howell Allchin)

In the second hand bookstore, she walks between stacks of old bindings, between paneled shelves (the underbark of emptiness, of let-go truths). A clock on the wall circles the day, and she falls in love (that simple, that fast) with the scent of leather and glue, with a man at the desk who folds and unfolds his hands.

What Becomes
>   (After *Montagne Sainte-Victoire* by Paul Cézanne)

It's the way things are. Banked in stillness, distant trees notch the wind. A wild bird hesitates between songs then flies into sunset (a kind of shining). Afraid of losing the earth and each other (whatever we're here to do), we move closer—walk, touch shoulders and hands, match our footsteps in small subliminal rhythms.

In the last light, one cloud becomes a mountain above the mountain. A flurry of bats becomes the Milky Way, and we make no pretense of understanding the infinite (deep inside us), our need to become nothing before we unname ourselves and disappear.

This Particular Light

                (After *The Sun* by Edvard Munch)

Weavers of the same place—beyond the body's dark containment, we entered the forest by our own choosing. Above us, galaxies pitched and sieved through air—another degree of second thought. Having used up all the words we knew for loneliness (and not sure what we found or what to call it), we considered options (as if happiness might be a choice). Finally, we returned to the larks' twill, the blue jays' liquid clicks—this life that is not about what things are but what they mean (all gift, and so much more than blood in the heart).

Do you remember the fox at twilight, the edge of the woods like a mirror in rain? Face it, there's only (ever) one whole note—the minor third, the perfect fifth—gratefully, we turn from the dark's protective depth into the brimmed burning of this particular light.

So Here You Are

(After *Spring* by Georgia O'Keeffe)

So here you are—by yourself because that's what you choose. Whether it's evening or late afternoon (more dark, more light) doesn't matter, the need to measure things becomes less and less important.

Lately, you think how life rushes through everything—unsettled dreams and things that will never happen again. Above snowmelt and bud, a weather vane turns (like old lies—sharply directional).

In a week or two, the lilacs will bloom; dogwoods will float like watered silk. It's ironic that all your seasons have led to reverence for things that move slowly; how you, like anything ordinary, changed without breaking.

A dog barks on the street behind you, the sound distantly familiar. Language. Landscape. In one of the trees, a small bird sings—this one bird's one song only for you because you are alone, and you hear it the way you can almost hear the time between breaths.

If There Is Such a Thing
(After *Woman by a Window Feeding Her Dog* by Mary Cassatt)

If there is such a thing as forever, I will be here by this high window, this dog beside me, sun on our faces. Everything important will spread out beneath us: gazebo and fountain. Each will be held in its own moment of beauty like the Yorkshire Terriers whose pictures hang on my kitchen wall: three no longer with me and this one who chews his rope giraffe to pieces with no regrets, no sentimental attachment— the chew worth whatever loss it incurs. Informed by his own spirit, he sees in things only things and wants nothing more than his leash and long walks, a game of throw the ball. He needs nothing more than to sleep on the floor between my feet or curled in the right angle my arm and elbow make when I hold him—the happiness he was made for.

If only forever were a choice we could make, I would choose this dog's world (and my place in it)—absolute innocence—no other life to plan for but this. Nothing but this: love without reservation—his world and mine as it ought to be and, in this moment, is.

The Way

                    (After *Night Scene* by Peter Paul Rubens)

Lately, they move in—their arms in our sleeves, hands in our gloves—less of us, more of them—*their* features on our changing faces, and it comes to us that they haven't let us go. It's the difference between gone and completely lost—they've always been there and come to us now like thoughts rethinking themselves.

Touchable again, they become the mirrors we hold to our lips—reflections of *them* look back at us through *our* eyes. We trace their heavy lids and wrinkled cheeks on the glass (what we loved in them, or didn't love enough—what we dread in ourselves). They come to remind us that there's more time past than there is ahead, and we walk with them inside their shadows. Softly, we call our own names into the dark—something to be clear about (proof of nothing).

Mother, father: where we began. Age brings them back to us in our own signs of change and impermanence. Strangely reassuring, this is the way they call us home, the way we begin to go.

Just Enough Spectacle
    (After *Snow Scene at Argenteuil* by Claude Monet)

It's that time—ice-sliver and ache—frost that feathers the sides of our eyes. This is the cold season, the winding down. When we were children, we imagined wolves in the woods, amber eyes between trees—excitement more than fear—a beauty that caught inside our breath, deep in the hope that took us there. Unaware of the ground beneath us, we walked into those woods (sometimes astonished), hands open inside our wooly mittens.

Childhood ponds skate into space; and, yes, this is winter—the calendar's last portion. Just past dawn, light flits over the top of things, like the end of another year seen through snow—just enough spectacle to offset time and age, to silence the "I" in who we've become.

Good Enough

(After *The Great Pine* by Paul Cézanne)

This one prefers her heroes flawed. Imperfect but tough, the right mix of metal and bread. One part hero, three parts imagination—always a bouquet of pine needles in his pocket. No surprises.

A rainy autumn brings us home to half-branches, another season without a map. The rain was already rain before we got here. No one stays. Wherever we're going (and we know this isn't it), there's not much point in perfection. Nothing is ever exactly what we think.

Wherever we are, the pines stay peaceful despite what the wind shakes loose—no thoughts, yours or mine, to disturb them. With evening coming on, shadows keep to themselves. The whole life of everything is all around us—what twilight shows (how we take it in). I know we intended to do better, but it just might be that we got it right after all, that what we've done is good enough.

As Far as Here Goes
    (After *The Soul of the Rose* by John William Waterhouse)

We know so little of things for which we pray. Humility. Forgiveness. And no idea what *soul* really means—its before and after, life after this…life…in timeless life—a vastness so remote we can't imagine it.

Morning, like light on the other side of frosted glass, clears into color. Starlings braid a pattern into the sky then vanish in what little time it takes to mark their flight. Beside me, a pinecone drops to the ground. This kind of purity comes to us without intention—in ordinary things that are anything but ordinary: the way sun lights a room at different angles, the way air moves behind us. It's about how *we* move, how we let the world twist through us as we twist through the world—like everything given to gravity—doing and doing.

And *here* (as far as here goes), it's about what doesn't separate us from ourselves—what's permanent, what's not. It's everything we turn toward—whatever signs we find of wonder and joy.

We Can Only Ask
                (After *Our Lady of Peace* by Evelyn de Morgan)

In a pause between dusk and full night, I walk where the path disappears. Among headstones, the worn Virgin is covered in moss, a granite angel has lost her hand. No knight, no armor (no heroes here). High in the cedars, sparrows gather—dispossessed—like prayers spoken in hopeless places.

Shadows stumble through light into deeper darkness, the stars' higher night picked out in reminders of our own brokenness (reminders of prayers sent to that place *where wings have memories of wings*, entireties so vast not even the stars understand them).

Blessèd are the poor in spirit—immeasurably blessed when the self is emptied and nothing remains. This isn't the place we come from—what matters isn't the battle but the return. We can only ask, and trust that we will be given as much as we need.

Like Wind Over Stones
    (After *The Rocks* by Vincent van Gogh)

I.

That night, I didn't look for answers or reasons. At the forest's edge, a bird rose over trees then held the high places with wings the way a soul reclaims its shape—awareness without thought.

II.

This morning began as a shifting distance: darkness stretched thin and peonies (from somewhere, the scent of peonies). Later, I waited while traffic stilled for a funeral—a desolate procession—corner to corner, the short space between time and eternity. I thought for a moment how we are chalk lost from a sidewalk, how much the air loves dust. And I thought how even death doesn't last—nothing lost in this illogical trust we call faith. Creation, redemption: twice (and ever) His. The white stag moves between worlds and always returns.

III.

Some things are easily remembered (resonant, indelible)—others, more fragile but equally blessed, are best understood by their loss. We have let ourselves be known slowly—beginning, being. So many years from where we were, we have spoken the word *open*.

IV.

Fragment to whole. Life is a skyward thing. It moves over us—like wind over stones—until we shine. And when we are ghosts (gone into what we believe), it will be more than the end of breathing (the end of water, the end of sky), as straightforward as this:

> flickers of air that rise up and leave as light.

THE PAINTINGS

I

Evening Wind
"Evening as Footnote"

By Edward Hopper (1882–1967)
1921
Etching
17.6 x 21 cm

In this Edward Hopper etching, a naked woman kneels on the edge of a bed. Long hair obscures her face as she turns her head toward an open window as if in surprise or fear at the sudden movement of the curtain billowing in. There are few details in the room, and space around the woman is spare, which, along with the stark black and white color palette, amplifies the power of the central figure and the painting's integration of time and place.

Children's Games
"How Things Were"

By Pieter Brueghel the Elder (c. 1525–1569)
1560
Oil on Panel
118 x 161 cm

This painting opens to a city center, a long street at the right, a stream at the left. Throughout the painting, over two hundred children (toddlers to adolescents) play leapfrog, roll hoops, stand on their heads, do handstands, walk on stilts, run a gauntlet, play blind man's bluff, enact tournaments, and participate in a host of other childhood amusements. They even carry their games into a civic building in the upper center of the square. The crowded scene is lavishly detailed and colored in bright tones of red, green, and blue set against a tan and brown background. One theory about this painting is that it uses children's games as a metaphor for adult follies and foolishness.

The Somnambulist
"What You See"

By Sir John Everett Millais (1829–1896)
1871
Oil on Canvas
60.6 x 35.8 cm

Facing the viewer with eyes averted, Millais's somnambulist walks barefoot on a sea-cliff path at nightfall. She wears a white Victorian-style nightgown; her hair is long and dark. A candle has gone out in the brass candleholder that hangs from her right hand. The sky is dark, the moon unseen. The effect of the woman's open-eyed stare and expressionless face are heightened by the painting's somber colors and implication of danger.

Winter Landscape
"Even When She Isn't Sure, She Is"

By Eugène Henri Paul Gauguin (1848–1903)
1879
Oil on Canvas
60.5 x 81 cm

This impressionist-style painting is a winterscape of a small village in Brittany. Cottages with snow-covered thatched roofs bring quiet triangular shapes into the foreground. Bare trees draw the eye upward toward the sky into which a Gothic steeple projects beyond view. Blurred shapes and muted colors bring various shades of white into focus and accent the aura of cold.

Woman before the Setting Sun
"Of What Is"

By Caspar David Friedrich (1744–1840)
1818-20
Oil on Canvas
23 x 30 cm

The single person in this painting is a woman in silhouette who stands with her back to the viewer as she looks into a reddish-yellow sky. The view is wide and includes a landscape that rises and falls around and in front of the woman. The impression is one of aloneness and, perhaps, a sense that the central figure looks into what was or what might have been.

Cats
"On Dit"

By Natalia Goncharova (1881–1962)
1913
Oil on Canvas
85.1 x 85.7 cm

In this Goncharova painting, which exemplifies the style that she and her collaborator Mikhail Larionov called Rayism, the viewer sees two (barely distinguishable) black cats with a tabby in between. The focus, in keeping with the style, does not depict the animals as we would see them but, rather, as the rays of light that reflect from their surfaces. Darts of color hint at the effects of light on the cats' coats and highlight the way adjoining surfaces reflect other color tones. The viewer experiences these cats almost as if they are in disguise.

Femme aux Phlox
"She Kept the Theory Going…"

By Albert Gleizes (1881–1953)
1910
Oil on Canvas
33 x 44 cm

With typical cubist treatment, the painting (also known as *Woman with Phlox* or *Woman with Flowers*) uses various shapes and forms to portray a woman who sits in an interior setting with vases of phlox in front of her and to her left. The window behind the woman opens to the outdoors; however, the lines between interior and exterior are indistinct. The color palette is restrained and powerfully monochromatic.

Man and Woman Contemplating the Moon
"This Almost Night"

By Caspar David Friedrich (1774–1840)
1824
Oil on Canvas
34 x 44 cm

A man and a woman stand on a steep path with their backs to the viewer. They are positioned to the left of the canvas center, and their clothing speaks of an earlier time. The woman's arm rests on the man's shoulder. Behind them, in the left foreground, is a large rock. To their right, a bare and partially uprooted tree overarches the scene. Its roots are exposed, and it leans away from the man and woman. There is another large rock beside the tree that also leans to the right. There are stones on the ground around the couple. A tall pine tree to the couple's right is full and green; however, like the entire composition, it is touched by shadows. A sliver of moon has risen in the distance in front of the couple and to their right. To the moon's right, and slightly above, is a star.

The Green Mirror
"Old Wine or Misfortune"

By Guy Rose (1867–1925)
1911
Oil on Canvas
81.28 x 100.33 cm

Seen from the back, a red-haired woman is seated in front of a large oval mirror. Dressed in a white nightdress and loosely draped emerald green robe, she holds a hand mirror to the side in her left hand, but her face is only seen in the larger mirror. Touches of green also appear in the mirror frame, in the carpet, and on a side table.

Enchantment (aka ***Cinderella***)
"Whatever Title We Gave It"

By Maxfield Parrish (1870–1966)
1913
Oil on Panel
Harper's Bazaar Cover, 1914

A young woman with long blonde hair stands on a staircase (Cinderella at midnight, just as the night's fairy tale enchantment is about to vanish). Her left arm and hand rest on the banister and her right hand is gently lifted at her right side. Her body faces the viewer, but her head is turned toward the stairs in front of her. A profusion of flowers dominates the upper right of the painting, and urns on the staircase are filled with the same flowers. The woman, staircase, and flowers are all depicted in radiant ocher tones. The background consists of stars scattered in a cobalt blue sky (the signature blue that was named for Parrish).

Lesbia and Her Sparrow
"It Doesn't Take Much"

By Sir Edward John Poynter (1836–1919)
1907
Oil on Canvas
49 x 37 cm

In this Pre-Raphaelite style painting, a Classical beauty, seated on a cushioned bench in a bower-like setting, looks at a sparrow perched on her right wrist. The sparrow looks back at the woman. Facing forward, she holds purple grapes in both hands, wears a purple robe over a sheer light gray gown, and has a wreath of violets in her hair. Associated in ancient times with Zeus (and, later, with spirituality), violets were made into crowns worn by poetry contest winners during Medieval times. Light pink roses (Victorian symbols of gentleness) also appear in the painting above the woman's left shoulder and in the bottom left foreground. Throughout, the principal colors are shades of purple, green, and cream. There is an open cage to the woman's left that suggests symbolic freedom.

Although it might be assumed that the name *Lesbia* was connected to sexual preferences, it was, in fact, a common Roman name and one chosen by the Latin poet Catullus whose tale of Lesbia and her sparrow was actually about his own lover Clodia Metelli (research suggests that he chose the name *Lesbia* because it had an identical metrical value to Clodia's).

Landscape: Garden Path
"As If That Place"

Marie Bracquemond (1840–1916)
Date Painted Unknown
Oil on Canvas
27 x 46 cm

Imagine a sunny day in spring or early summer. Neatly planted flowers grow on each side of a golden yellow path that is bordered by a low decorative border; a few of the flowers' shadows lie quietly on the path. There is a sense of order and light that reaches into even the tree-shaded parts of the scene. In addition to the yellow path, the dominant colors are tones of green, red, and white (with a few touches of dusky pink). The scene is so carefully detailed that the viewer can almost feel the warmth of the sun on the garden path—warmth that doesn't diminish as the path moves into the distance.

II

The Wave
"For a Moment, Like Stones"

By Pierre-August Renoir (1841–1919)
1882
Oil on Canvas
53.9 x 65 cm

This painting's focus is the startling immediacy and the dynamic transience of a wave as it crashes onto the shore. Renoir's use of a palette knife has created an impasto (paint laid on the canvas very thickly to provide texture and emphasis) of roiling foam, sand, and mist. The colors are muted creams, blues, greens, and yellows, with touches of red.

The False Mirror
"Seeing and Seeing"

By René Magritte (1898–1967)
1928
Oil on Canvas
54 x 80.9 cm

The False Mirror is a surrealist work in which a giant, lashless eye with a solid, black pupil dominates the center. The iris consists of blue, cloud-filled sky. In a tricky duality, the viewer looks through the eye in much the same way that one would look through a window; at the same time, the eye looks at the viewer. The painting challenges the viewer to question what he or she is seeing—what isn't and what is.

Beech Grove
"If I'm Searching Again"

By Gustav Klimt (1862–1918)
1902
Oil on Canvas
100 x 100 cm

In this landscape from symbolist Gustav Klimt's golden phase (in which some paintings included gold leaf) bare birch trees appear in grey-blue with fallen leaves scattered on the ground beneath them. There is blue sky behind the trees in the upper quarter of the image. The painting is stark and touched by a sense of change and loss. Although the trees and leaves are finely detailed, the painting itself is comprised only of the small patch of sky, the beech trees, and the fallen leaves.

Beata Beatrix
"In Memory Of"

By Dante Gabriel Rossetti (1828–1882)
c. 1864–1870
Oil on Canvas
86.4 x 66 cm

Painted by Pre-Raphaelite founder Dane Gabriel Rossetti, the model for this painting was his wife Elizabeth Siddal. The title means "Blessed Beatrice," and Rossetti cast his wife (an apparent suicide) in the role of Dante's thirteenth century "La Vita Nuova"—the greatly desired but unattainable love. Smaller and above the central figure, are Dante (to the right) and an angel (to the left). In the distance the Ponte Vecchio (bridge) denotes the city of Florence, Italy. The aspect of the painting is misty and transcendent; the effect is haunting. Rossetti wrote in a letter that he depicted his Beatrice in a state of "spiritual transformation." The death imagery in this work is powerful. A red dove drops a white poppy (a symbol of death) into Beatrice's outstretched hands. Her eyes are closed, her lips slightly parted. There is a sundial near Beatrice's left shoulder. The colors are dark: muted red, green, and brown, with patches of light just above the woman's head, on the woman's face, on the sundial, and on the dove.

A Family
"Because This Name Will Stop with Me..."

By Louis le Brocquy (1916–2012)
1951
Oil on Canvas
147 x 185 cm

In this representation of a family, the mother is nude and leans on one arm as she lies on a table. She faces the viewer, but her eyes appear to be closed. A cat peeks out of the sheet that partially covers the woman. In the background the father sits with his back bent and his head bowed. To the right a small child holds a bouquet of flowers. Somberly portrayed, the three figures are set in a barren room that is lit by a bare light bulb. From the artist's "grey period," the painting's palette is comprised of predominantly grays and whites with only the child's bouquet to introduce a note of color.

Mountain Landscape with Bridge
"Once, Late in the Day"

By Thomas Gainsborough (1727–1788)
c. 1783–84
Oil on Canvas
113 x 133.4 cm

Gainsborough's landscape includes people, paths, a river, a bridge, a mountain (in the left background), and a rustic house (in the far mid-right). A pastoral scene and idyllic topography are key features. Mountains to the left and right of the bridge frame the view like curtains that add depth and dimension to the small and featureless figures seen crossing the bridge. Creamy clouds float in a sky that rises above the bridge and river. The palette is primarily muted blues, greens, and brown. Most striking is the way in which the viewer's eyes are led through fore and middle grounds—past river, bridge, and mountain—into a distance where the quality of light speaks to something ethereal and otherworldly.

Ophelia
"Just Perhaps"

By John Everett Millais (1829–1896)
1851–1852
Oil on Canvas
76.2 x 111.8 cm

John Everett Millais, who painted this version of a popular Victorian subject, was one of three Pre-Raphaelite Brotherhood founders (along with Dante Gabriel Rossetti and Holman Hunt). The painting speaks to death in meticulous detail and with an almost cinematic intensity. In Shakespeare's *Hamlet*, Ophelia's death takes place offstage, but is described by Gertrude. Millais's attention to botanic detail is significant in this work and includes the plants mentioned by Gertrude in Shakespeare's play; among them are willow, daisy, nettle, violets, and pansies. These flowers also endorse the deeply symbolic vocabulary of Victorian flower language. Ophelia lies in a stream; her skirt billows around her. Her eyes and mouth are open; her hands are just above the water's surface, palms turned up. The viewer questions whether she jumped or fell and whether or not she is still alive as she is seen in the painting. There is a poppy among the flowers in her hand (a symbol of death) that also appeared in Rossetti's *Beata Beatrix*. Ironically, the model for this painting was Elizabeth Siddal, who was also the model for *Beata*.

The Weeping Woman
"The Part"

By Pablo Picasso (1881–1973)
1937
Oil on Canvas
60 x 49 cm

Picasso's *Weeping Woman* depicts the face of a crying woman whose anguish is virtually tangible. Surrealist in essence, the painting presents an image of suffering painted in the artist's early "analytical cubist" style. The woman's face is shown in angular, overlying fragments that speak to brokenness. The kaleidoscopic effect of line and form colored in red, yellow, green, blue, orange, and brown is interrupted by jagged black lines in the center of the woman's face, mouth, and chin. The handkerchief that she wedges into her mouth has the look of broken glass.

Forget Me Not
"Pieces"

By Arthur Hughes (1832–1915)
1901–1902
Oil on Canvas
108 x 64 cm

The central image in this painting is a young woman. The setting is medieval, and the woman kneels before a large, brass-studded trunk. Lying on her bed to the right are a lute and a bow. The padded headboard, complete with Gothic finials and a pair of embroidered angels, is inscribed "*Deus Magnificat.*" On the floor to her left, a bouquet of small flowers lies on a cap (the kind worn by medieval men). The woman wears a bright blue cape with a white dress beneath. Her hair is blonde, and she looks upward toward a casement window. Only two panes of the window are visible, but the last of the evening light illuminates her face. In her hands, she holds a sprig of forget me nots.

Flaming June
"What She's Always Known"

By Sir Frederic Leighton (1830–1896)
1895
Oil on Canvas
120 x 120 cm

In this Pre-Raphaelite style painting, a sleeping woman dressed in a vivid semi-transparent orange gown lies asleep on a classically inspired marble bench that is heavily draped with fabric. Rounded into herself—a circular shape on a square canvas—the woman, like a sleeping carousel of color and form, is said to be reminiscent of Michelangelo's figure *Night*. Her gown both reveals and conceals her body. Above and behind the woman, a shimmering sea floats on a high horizon line. An oleander flower lies on a shelf above and to the right of the woman's head. Highly toxic, the oleander's Victorian flower meaning was "caution" or "beware."

Head of an Angel (After Rembrandt)
"Poem about Angels That Begins with a Sump Pump"

By Vincent van Gogh (1853–1890)
1889
Oil on Canvas
64 x 54 cm

Here, an angel (similar to one painted by Rembrandt in *Jacob Wrestling the Angel*) faces downward, away from the viewer, with eyes closed. Its left arm reaches toward the viewer, but the palm is tightly clenched. The angel's wings are outstretched and extend beyond the canvas. Also called *Half Figure of an Angel*, the painting is distinguished by van Gogh's clear brush strokes and vibrant shades of blue touched with white. Portrayed with a yellow tinted halo, the angel isn't represented as young and beautiful. Most striking is the way van Gogh painted light into darkness, creating with oils the look of watercolors and imbuing the image with a seraphic impression that is equally worldly and mystical.

Starry Night
"Moment and Memory"

By Jean-François Millet (1814–1875)
c. 1850–1865
Oil on Canvas
65.4 x 81.3 cm

One of the Barbizon School founders, Millet painted a dark landscape with a few trees projecting into the night sky. The sky is filled with stars, including three shooting stars. In the center of the horizon line, there is a small area of muted light. Known primarily for his depictions of peasant farmers working in fields, this painting suggests another of Millet's repeated themes: how divinity may be found in the simplest of subjects.

III

Epiphany
"Simply Here"

By Max Ernst (1891–1976)
1940
Oil on Canvas
54 x 65 cm

Ernst's *Epiphany* emerged from a disordered and dangerous time in the artist's life and depicts a chaotic and surrealistic interpretation of the Magi's visit to Bethlehem. The imagery is nightmarishly dream-like. Grotesque animal forms that blend into tree-like images, a small round star in the upper left, and a bizarre Magus suggest allegory and symbolism, and perhaps hint at something in the relationship between nature and humanity. The sky is eerily green, and the human and animal images are depicted in dark tones of brown and umber.

All Souls' Day
"Where the Dead Are Strangers"

By Jakub Schikaneder (1855–1924)
1888
Oil on Canvas
139.5 x 220 cm

All Souls' Day is celebrated in the Christian Church on November 2nd, following All Hallow's Eve (October 31st), and All Saints' Day (November 1st). In this realist painting, an elderly woman stands with her back against a cemetery wall. A tomb behind her holds a wreath and a lamp with reddish glass panes. The woman wears a black shawl with a long red and white skirt underneath. A headscarf is tied under her chin in babushka style. Head down and turned to the viewer's left, she supports herself with a cane in her right hand. Scattered on the grass, at the woman's feet and around her, are fallen leaves. To her right are a stone slab and a bare, fallen branch.

Lake with Dead Trees
"Past the Waterline"

By Thomas Cole (1801–1848)
1825
Oil on Canvas
85.7 x 68.6 cm

This Hudson River School landscape depicts a lake that is bordered by mountains in the background and ringed with dead trees. The topography's barrenness is both picturesque and unsettling. The tree line touches a sky that is darkly clouded on the left with a patch of blue and light (above the tree line) on the right. There is a strong sense of movement in the falling and receding storm clouds, as well as in two deer in the lower mid-foreground. The deer on the left stands still and looks at the viewer while the other faces right and is poised to run away.

Pilgrim at the Gate of Idleness
"For a Long Time"

By Sir Edward Coley Burne-Jones (1833–1898)
1884
Oil on Canvas
95.5 x101 cm

Loosely based on Chaucer's "Roumant de la Rose," this allegorical painting is part of a trilogy by one of the leading Pre-Raphaelite artists. Trees stand in the background, and a medieval structure appears to the right, along with a rectangular water feature at its base. The two central figures are dressed in muted green and brown medieval attire: idleness (in the guise of a lovely young woman wearing a circlet of roses in her hair) reaches toward a pilgrim with her right hand outstretched. The pilgrim's upturned hands suggest resistance to temptation and determination to struggle toward victory in finding love (symbolized in the Burne-Jones trilogy of the briar rose). During the Victorian era, the rose was a popular floral emblem and took on various meanings. Burne-Jones added to the lexicon with his "rose paintings" in which roses symbolized the heart's desire.

Tintagel on the Cornish Coast
"Shooting Stars"

By William Trost Richards (1833–1905)
1883
Oil on Canvas
57.15 x 93.98 cm

Tintagel Castle, located on the Cornish coast in England, is the legendary birthplace of King Arthur. Now in ruins, it remains a romantic, mystical place. This painting shows Tintagel high on its headland with the Atlantic Ocean crashing on the rocks beneath it. A higher cliff stands to the left. Seabirds fly overhead and to the right. The principal colors are shades of blue, green, and brown. From the silence of the painting comes an almost-heard sense of crashing waves and sea gulls' cries.

Still Life with an Open Book and Spectacles
"A Man at the Desk"

By William T. Howell Allchin (1844–1883)
c. 1863–70
Oil on Canvas
14.9 x 20 cm

An old book opened to Shakespeare's *Timon of Athens* and a pair of eyeglasses placed on the left side page of the open book are all the viewer sees in this painting. Colored in sepia tones, the bottom corner of the left-hand page is turned up, as is the (slightly less turned-up) bottom of the right-side page, giving the impression (along with the glasses) that the reader has read a few pages and stopped.

Montagne Sainte-Victoire
"What Becomes"

By Paul Cézanne (1830–1906)
1890–1895
Oil on Canvas
55 x 65.40 cm

Montagne Sainte-Victoire is a mountain in southern France that overlooks Aix-en-Provence. It became the subject of a number of Cézanne's paintings. This depiction is clearly a winter landscape dominated by the mountain in the central background. The sky is filled with clouds. To the right, the trunk and branches of a bare tree are outlined in dark slate blue; the entire color palette is muted and features shades of light blue, cream, and faded ochre (the latter mainly in the village and fields in the foreground).

The Sun
"This Particular Light"

By Edvard Munch (1863–1944)
1911–1916
Oil on Canvas
455 x 780 cm

The dominant image in this painting (one of several versions) is a central sun (strangely, in the shape of a light bulb) that throws shafts of yellow, red, and blue light over the sea, the bleak rocks of a barren landscape, and a small piece of green land between the sea and the rocks. The dynamism and centrality of the sun suggest a metaphysical presence and give the painting an enigmatic complexity.

Spring
"So Here You Are"

By Georgia O'Keeffe (1887–1986)
1923–24
Oil on Canvas
45.7 x 35.4 cm

Colored in pastel shades of lavender, green, blue, white, and gray, this painting is O'Keeffe's treatment of a subject that her husband Alfred Stieglitz photographed around the same time. In comparison to the photograph, O'Keeffe simplified the building (which held her husband's darkroom at Lake George) by omitting such details as the chimney, window, and horizontal siding. In O'Keeffe's painting, blue sky, white clouds, and pink and white spring blossoms frame the building at the sides and top; green grass fills the foreground. The lower part of an elongated flagpole stands in front of, and to the left. Electrical wires stretch upward from the right, and a black weather vane sits at the peak of the building's roof.

Woman by a Window Feeding Her Dog
"If There Is Such a Thing"

By Mary Cassatt (1844–1926)
1880
Oil, Gouache and Pastel on Paper, Laid Down on Canvas
60.96 x 41.28 cm

Mary Cassatt, an American impressionist, offers the viewer a moment in time and place as a seated woman, seen from the right and looking down at her hands, prepares to give her dog a bit of food. To the woman's left, a window opens to sunlight. A dog with a small face and pointed ears looks up at the woman in anticipation of the treat in her hands. With the exception of the window's yellow light as background and its reflection on the woman and dog, the color palette is comprised of rich ocher tones. There is an aura of serenity in the painting and a sense of peaceful connection in the bond between woman and dog.

Night Scene
"The Way"

By Peter Paul Rubens (1577–1640)
c. 1616–1617
Oil on Panel
79 x 64 cm

In this Flemish Baroque genre painting, a young boy lights a candle from one already lit and held by an old man. Their faces (which are central to the painting) are intensely lit by candlelight, their clothing is richly colored, and there is a dramatic element in the work that is typical of its era. The meticulously rendered details of age and youth in the central figures' faces are strongly underscored by the apparent symbolism of the youth reaching to light his fresh candle from the lit and diminished candle in the old man's hand.

Snow Scene at Argenteuil
"Just Enough Spectacle"

By Claude Monet (1840–1926)
1875
Oil on Canvas
71 x 91 cm

An extraordinarily snowy winter during 1874–75 motivated Monet to paint eighteen Argenteuil snowscapes. This one (among others) focuses on the Boulevard Saint-Denis where Monet lived. The viewer looks down the boulevard towards the Seine. A couple walks through the snow (almost lost in it), and other small, undefined figures are seen in the distance. Atmosphere rather than detail directs the view, which is depicted in a palette of blues and grays. The smallness of people in this painting contrasts significantly to the larger vision of winter's bleakness.

The Great Pine
"Good Enough"

By Paul Cézanne (1830–1906)
1887–89
Oil on Canvas
84 x 92 cm

The trunk and branches of this painting's central pine tree were drawn in dark outline and then painted in with color and shadow. Rust and yellow on the ground from which the tree rises give a sense of autumn. The tree's canopy is dominated by thick brush strokes with a blue sky in the background. Despite the dark trees around the central pine, and the pine itself, white areas of sky emphasize the tree's presence and give the painting a sense of light.

The Soul of the Rose
"As Far as Here Goes"

By John William Waterhouse (1849–1917)
1908
Oil on Canvas
88.3 x 59.1 cm

In this painting, informed by Pre-Raphaelite style and sensibility, the central figure is a young woman. The viewer sees her from the left side—to just below her waist. Her thick red hair is entwined with pearls and styled in a chignon. She leans against a garden wall to inhale the fragrance of a deep pink rose that she holds in her right hand. In Victorian flower language, dark pink roses were symbols of gratitude. The woman's skin is flushed, her neck is stretched upward; her left hand is pressed against the wall. Portrayed with great delicacy, the woman is depicted in warm colors; her hair and skin tones are complemented by blends of pinks and earthy oranges, greens, and browns. Clothed in a loosely flowing garment patterned in subtle blues and gold, the woman's graceful form and the rose in her hand are set in juxtaposition to the solidity of the wall in front of her. There is a sense of the transitory in the painting—youth, beauty, the rose, and life itself.

Our Lady of Peace
"We Can Only Ask"

By Evelyn de Morgan (1855–1919)
1907
Oil on Canvas
191.1 x 96.5 cm

Pre-Raphaelite influence and medieval design elements (principally chivalry and Marian devotion) dominate this painting in which a young knight kneels in prayer before a vision of the Virgin Mary. The Virgin is robed in white and garlanded with olive branches—the personification of peace. She appears in a rainbow of light along with a group of cherubim. Her arms are raised in gentle benediction. The knight's prayerful pose is met with the Virgin Mary's expression of quiet sadness. Although the two figures are closely placed in this painting, they do not look at each other directly. An architectural element to the left appears in the form of a column carved with grape vines (symbolic of Holy Communion and Christ's sacrificial blood). A lizard, a snake, and a bird also appear on the column. The painting contains suggestions of faith, of the futility of war, and of longing not fulfilled. Overall, however, there is an abiding reminder of hope.

The Rocks
"Like Wind Over Stone"

By Vincent van Gogh (1853–1890)
1888
Oil on Canvas
54.9 x 65.7 cm

This painting depicts a rocky, windswept landscape. There is an emotional presence in the composition dramatized by the artist's use of greens, blues, and yellows applied in bold brushstrokes and thick streaks of color. The composition is comprised of craggy stones that move upward toward a wind-twisted oak tree that rises in the center and dominates the canvas with dark leaves set against a pale sky. Layers of paint offer an almost sculptural dimension, along with a striking linear quality.

NOTES

"How Things Were"—Reference is made to a film called *Duck and Cover* that was shown during the early 1950s in elementary schools to teach children how to protect themselves ("duck and cover") during a bombing or at the first sound of a warning siren. Children were taught to duck in order to avoid glass and anything else that might fly through the air and then to take cover under their desks or in hallways away from windows. Just as fire drills are common today, so were these "drills" during the early 1950s.

"On Dit"—*On dit* is a French term that means, literally, "It is said, they say." More loosely translated, it means a bit of gossip or a vague rumor.

"If I'm Searching Again"—In memory of Gail Gerwin.

"Because This Name Will Stop with Me"—In memory of my father, William J. Kenny, Jr. Aengus and Oisín are characters in Irish legend and myth.

"Just Perhaps"—In memory of Les Price.

"Pieces"—In memory of my mother, Adele Petro Kenny.

"What She's Always Known"—In memory of Linda Radice.

"Shooting Stars"—The line that begins *"As it was in the beginning,"* is part of a doxology addressed to the three Divine Persons of the Trinity. Colloquially known as the "Glory Be," it appears in various Christian rites as follows: *Glory be to the Father, and to the Son, and to the Holy Spirit, as it was in the beginning, is now, and ever shall be, world without end. Amen.*

"If There Is Such a Thing"—Remembering Dylan (1976–1993), Yeats (1993–2008), and Bijou (1994-2011), and for Chaucer (2011–), my Yorkshire Terriers.

"Good Enough"—For Bob Fiorellino.

"As Far As Here Goes"—The quoted (italicized) part of the first line is a loose translation of Geoffrey Chaucer's *We witen nat what thing we preyen heere* from "The Knight's Tale."

"We Can Only Ask"—A poem with lines from William Butler Yeats and St. Matthew. Yeats: *where wings have memories of wings* (from "Upon a House Shaken by the Land Agitation"). St. Matthew: *Blessed are the poor in spirit* (from Matthew 5:3, the Beatitudes).

"Like Wind Over Stones"—For Alex Pinto. White deer figure in the mythologies of many cultures. The white hart mentioned in this poem refers to a mystical creature that the ancients believed could move between the earthly and spiritual worlds. In Celtic mythology, it was an indicator that the Otherworld was near. To later Christians, the white hart came to symbolize Christ. In Arthurian legend, the white hart was always able to evade capture, and its pursuit represented humankind's spiritual quest.

ACKNOWLEDGMENTS

Grateful acknowledgment is made to the editors of the following print and online journals, anthologies, and books in which some of these poems have appeared or are forthcoming, in current or earlier forms, some with different titles.

A Lightness, A Thirst, or Nothing at All (Welcome Rain Publishers, 2015)—"Just Perhaps"

California Quarterly—"In Memory Of"

Exit 13 Magazine—"Shooting Stars"

Ibbetson Street—"Evening As Footnote" and "Simply Here"

Life and Legends—"Just Perhaps"

Lips—"For A Long Time," "How Things Were," "If I'm Searching Again," "As If That Place," and "So Here You Are"

NJARTform—"Where the Dead Are Strangers"

Paterson Literary Review—"Pieces," "The Way," "If There Is Such a Thing" (under the title "This"), "Poem about Angels that Begins with a Sump Pump," and "The Part"

Persimmon Tree—"Old Wine or Misfortune"

Ragazine—"On Dit" and "Past the Waterline"

Schuylkill Valley Journal—"This Almost Night"

Schuylkill Valley Journal Online (Issue #5)—"This Almost Night"

Shot Glass Journal—"Even When She Isn't Sure, She Is," "What You See," and "Where the Dead Are Strangers"

Shrew, A Literary Zine—"For a Moment, Like Stones" and "As far As Here Goes"

Stillwater Review—"Because this Name Will Stop with Me," "Of What Is," "Once, Late in the Day," "What She's Always Known," "Seeing and Seeing," and "What Becomes"

The Crafty Poet II (Terrapin Books, 2016)—"Pieces"

The Good Men Project—"Just Enough Spectacle"

U.S. 1 Worksheets—"A Man at the Desk," "She Kept the Theory Going," and "Moment and Memory"

Voices from Here 2 (Paulinskill Poetry Project, Anthology)—"Whatever Title We Gave It"

What Matters (Welcome Rain Publishers, 2011)—"In Memory Of"

Your Daily Poem—"If There Is Such a Thing"

"Old Wine or Misfortune" was a winning poem in the *Persimmon Tree* East Coast States Competition (2015)

The following poems received Pushcart Prize nominations: "Shooting Stars" (*Exit 13 Magazine*, 2015), "Because This Name Will Stop with Me" (*Stillwater Review*, 2015), "For a Long Time" (*Lips*, 2016), "Pieces" (*Paterson Literary Review* 2016), and "Even When She Isn't Sure, She Is" (*Shot Glass Journal*, 2017).

"The Way" received honorable mention in the 2017 Allen Ginsberg Awards.

Sincerest thanks go to my publisher John Weber for being the considerate and generous publisher that he is; and special acknowledgment goes to my editor and friend Charles DeFanti for his unfailing friendship and guidance since 1966.

ABOUT THE AUTHOR

Adele Kenny, founding director of the Carriage House Poetry Series, and poetry editor of *Tiferet Journal*, is a poet and nonfiction writer whose poems, articles, and reviews have been widely published throughout the U.S. and abroad. She is the recipient of two NJ State Arts Council poetry fellowships, several agency-sponsored writing grants, first place Merit Book Award, first place Henderson Award, Merton Poetry of the Sacred Award, Writer's Digest Poetry Award, the International Book Award for Poetry, a Women of Excellence Award for her work in the arts and humanities (Union County, NJ Commission on the Status of Women), and Kean University's Distinguished Alumni Award. She has been Poet Laureate of Fanwood, NJ since 2012. Her book *A Lightness, A Thirst, or Nothing at All* was a 2016 Paterson Poetry Prize finalist. A former creative writing professor in the College of New Rochelle's Graduate School, and former report writing instructor at the John H. Stamler Police Academy, she has read her poetry in the U.S., England, France, and Ireland, and has twice been a Geraldine R. Dodge Festival poet.

Website: www.adelekenny.com
Poetry Blog: www.adelekenny.blogspot.com

www.ingramcontent.com/pod-product-compliance
Lightning Source LLC
Chambersburg PA
CBHW032207040426
42449CB00005B/483